Dido in Winter

ALSO BY ANNE SHAW

Undertow
(winner of the Lexi Rudnitsky First Book Prize in Poetry)

DIDO in Winter

POEMS

Anne Shaw

A Karen & Michael Braziller Book

PERSEA BOOKS / NEW YORK

Thanks to the Lexi Rudnitsky Poetry Project
for its continuing support of winners
of the Lexi Rudnitsky First Book Prize.

Persea Books, Inc.
277 Broadway
New York, NY 10007

Library of Congress Cataloging-in-Publication Data
Shaw, Anne (Anne Meads).
[Poems. Selections]
Dido in winter : poems / Anne Shaw. — First edition.
       pages cm
ISBN 978-0-89255-429-4 (original trade paperback : alk. paper)
I. Title.
PS3619.H3916A6 2014
811'.6–dc23
          2013042147

First edition
Printed in the United States of America
Designed by Rita Lascaro

for a
the first letter

ACKNOWLEDGEMENTS

Grateful acknowledgement is made to the following publications in which poems in this book first appeared:

Barrow Street, Black Warrior Review, Columbia: A Journal of Literature and Art, Copper Nickel, Crab Orchard Review, Crazy Horse, Denver Quarterly, Diode, Greensboro Review, Hotel Amerika, Horse Less Review, Indiana Review, Inter|rupture, Literary Imagination, Massachusetts Review, Meridian, New American Writing, New Orleans Review, Tuesday: An Art Project, Vinyl Poetry, Water~Stone Review, We Are So Happy to Know Something, West Branch, Wired

"City You Won't Come Back To" appeared on *Verse Daily, Wisconsin Poets' Calendar,* and on ExpressMilwaukee.com.

"Dido to the Little Matchgirl" appeared in *A Face to Meet the Faces: An Anthology of Contemporary Persona Poetry.*

For generous feedback, material support, and disaster prevention, deep gratitude to Traci Brimhall, Mary Crow, Nick Demske, Kate Siner Francis, Riley Kins, Alane Spinney, Dianne Timblin, and the rest of the Posse.

Warm thanks to the Lexi Rudnitsky Poetry Project for their continued support, and to Rita Lascaro for her beautiful design despite the quirks and challenges of this manuscript. I am also grateful to Brett Hall for a fellowship at the Squaw Valley Community of Writers, where a number of these poems were written. Most of all, thanks to my editor, Gabriel Fried, for his humor, patience, insight, and ongoing belief in the work.

CONTENTS

iv.

v.

vi.

Dido in Winter

INVITATION

Voices drift across the lawn
and form in the shape of clovers. A slight breeze
bezels the fishpond, lens
of grainy light, black

cord covered with electric tape. Kneel
on the concrete. Tile, sedge.

Koi ghost out
to meet you, blunt-
edged hunger curving
blindly up.

Take this bract that rises and subsides.

Butterscotch or red and white,
their bodies slick
as sorrow, lathered
with the cold, unseemly weed.

Elsewhere, there's a party.
Clink of glasses, square of kitchen light.

Elsewhere, a pair of pliers
spreads
its implicate beak.
A hooded sweatshirt
gestures from the bottom of a lake.

Here, put these on. You're going to need
the leather gloves I tossed off in the shed.

Speech is just an instrument to register
the night. I offer

you no hook, no tool,
nothing to make fast

no metal implement with which to cut or mend.

Some Things She Kept While Some She Kept Apart

Her hand on the faucet, turning
    the water off, then on again
        as she waits for the cold to turn hot.
In the stream, her fingers flicker and the sky
    grows lighter, nightclouds moving west.
    She's risen again at this hour, fulcrum
        of the day. She hears the brief susurrus of the wind,
the ragged barks of dogs, and the low hoot of the bird,
        and the bird, is it *mourning*
    or *morning*, grief in its ashy plume,
        or timeclock, cool and stricken
            some ghost-beast of a mechanistic sky?

Who sees her in this kitchen, the burner flaring blue,
    rinse of light through the window, green tea
        growing stronger in her cup?
Is it you there, reader, sly voyeur, glimpsing her coyly
    through your one-way page? Will you call her
    though you do not know her name, Emily
        or Salomé or Jade? Or decide as she sits alone,
that she and I are one, that you and I are, or that you and she?
        (Such is the small equivalence we teach ourselves to make
        though she sighs and grows suspicious, moves
        to another room
            in another part of the house we cannot see.)

And now the city's growing plain,
     the grey expanse of lake
          less gorgeous than in halflight.
As when you walk the park
     at twilight and the trees are full of nests.
     For it's dusk now, and the day has slid away
          and the woman that you were is nowhere to be found
except in recollection's rough-hewn cave.
          There's a black form in the branches,
     the shape of a cat: an owl
     and you pause beneath the scrub tree where it sits
attentive for the scuffle of its prey (mouse
          that carves its thin path through the grass
               before it breaks for open air, clipped lawn—)
                    An owl whose square and tufted head turns
                    in silhouette,

as it sees you more precisely than you will ever see—
     in night vision goggles, perhaps, unearthly glow of green,
          perhaps in outline, white against the black, your phantom-body
moving in your coat. You feel its pupils narrow
     as it sizes you, flies off. That way of coming into, being known. It's a way
     of being broken. There are so many ways:
          One wet glove on the pavement, or a man who lingers
               on his balcony
watching the red and purple city lights. Or the body's restless rise,
                    its falling-back. The truss of waking,
          and the truss of sleep. Or the orange within the orange, that small
     and bitter fruit
          called *navel*, that a woman eats, the blossom
               of a bruise across her thigh. (Say *fist*

or *rapist, solitude* or *brood*—) But you are not this woman.
      You refuse. Her memory flakes off, white chips of paint
           through the dark and flooded runnels of the mind.
So we make, of recollection, an old formica table spread with books. Silence,
        or a wreath of silences. (Smoke woven
            through the halflight of the bar,
   and the low thump of a drumkit through the walls
               in the next apartment over, where you sit
             you there, reader, toying with resolve,
     with premise, with a list of premises: Not to be done
            with waking. Not to be done with the work:
                this making and remaking of a mind—)

The way, in summer, yellowjackets
      swirl around the carnage of sweet trash
          radiant, aglow in summer heat.
How the raw smell opens upward,
      bright and intricate as sex. No.
     what comes before sex: cough
          through the open window, shoe kicked toward the floor,
and then, as if unbearable, the slow intake of breath
          how the self curls back
before it splits—as flesh does
      when it parts from flesh: Yes,
          that pink anemone, that seahorse glint.

ANOTHER ART HOUSE MOVIE

A rule of sun falls inward across the table:
What craft in the ivory grapes, what ugly crap.
You are always already moving, whatever pants you wear:
Corduroy trousers, my poor pale friend, or simple water pooling in its glass.

Drink it. Close the door after. Aprons, pens, your voice,
And all the rest. It's a malleable hour
In the middle of the day. An edgy lottery writhes your sleep,
A cicada creeps like an infant to its birth.

Meanwhile, your shadow elongates and slips through the summer grass.
The door of the boathouse opens; the footsteps of a boy
Resonate at certain frequencies. Your room is a room
In shambles: a table set with stones, a steaming pan, a nail, a crust of bread;

His hand with tiny cuts; a boat, recurrent flower blooming in its thimble—

HOUSE

We did not ask each other questions.
The night was clean, it was spare.
Doorways opened before us.

I took you by the hand. We ran
up a narrow stair
to the inmost room. The floor

was fleshed in lamplight. Then globes
burst open, shattered. The thin
walls shook and were still.

The chairs
leaned out of their shadows
elsewhere in the house . . .

Downstairs,
in the kitchen, the page
of the calendar rustled, turned

on its wire hinge.

ALCOVE

i.

Stricture of these braided days
this sadness that I love   knots of water
coursing through the dam

As the dog runs through the underbrush
his motion is a current, and he moves
as if to move were a simple act of will—

And all my wildness reined in.

>   *Deny the redwing's trill*
>   *Deny the white root swollen in the ground*

ii.

How the river glints like metal   these residues
of speech   my life
returned to me   I don't know why—

iii.

Then grant me sleeping and waking
form of your hands on my shoulders
or careless on my body as you sleep

Grant me a morning of you
—pears, black coffee, the paper—
splints of sunlight moving on the floor

Allow the dark entanglements
the river fire green, the moon aghast
reined in the asking wind—

Grant me a season only
pasture me a day: an alcove
carved of olive wood   wherein

we may converse   let silence
drop   let quiet
enter in

Unruly Clock.

How strangely things unmoor themselves.
For instance, overhead: shadow of a bird
without a bird. As paint peels back
from the porch front, cloud-thread
raveled out against the blue. How my body
craves extinction. Yours, a tenderness.
On top of or below. As the preposition
wanders from its noun. The lip
and its restriction. You, the fricative angel
in my bed. How a bulb turns on
in the farmhouse: a private
radiance. And the body's rapt attention,
apparent slips of tongue. Some truths
I kidnap back into the dark. My realm
of unbecoming, kingdom of shatter and thrust. Fields
in the side view plated now with water over loam.
The little clatter the mind makes, and each
peculiar crevice of a heart. Such beds of flood
and thistle: their many endings, turnings,
passings-through. Then all my slick retractions
flattering a passage through the skull. There is luck
and luck's remission, there are freckled hands
on locks, tallow-meshes hanging in the trees. And the bees
relentless, hungry now, summer or its semblance
bent in sad arrival, creeping charlie tiny in the lawn—

City You Won't Come Back To

A white light strafes the railyard as freight trains churn and click

past burned-out tanneries, car yoked to car. Slow halt of a body as it grinds

to the brink of rails. What flashes to beguile. What we let go by. Tonight

we sit in the diner, red block letters pulsing in our spoons. In the black sheets

of the windows, we study the reflection of reflection. If I put my hand

on your hand. If you put your head on your chest. If I took up the sugar

and poured it on your plate, saying *start anew*. Pay the tab and then we will resign:

the tangleyard benighted with belief, the season saddled roughly to its twinge.

Nightshade roots in the alley, boxwood snares the park. All that rust
   and stubble,

all that riff and tear. For now, let's walk where elm trees net the vacant lot.

For now, let's traipse out barefoot, gummy tarmac blackening our heels.

BIRD & HAND

Listen: you are an eyesore glitzy
as a billboard my bluelight
special baby my-shiny-in-the-rain
but the heart is a homey summer

slippy as a raw egg on my plate
crumped open like a torso my
bloody clementine pitched
on the tarmac under the jizz of stars

and the street's gone vacant vagrant
the lawn unmown the lawn
a little forest a little savagery
like the one between us darling

a bird trapped in the house
banging and banging and when I
opened my fist to the blueblack
it was already gone

Panopticon

1.

There is rain and there is city
and a woman eating toast. There is honey
in her mouth and bread, a black and bitter cup.

In the kitchen there are peonies and cans of broth and meat.

    Where sunlight puzzles its pieces on the floor.

2.

A glass dish shaped like rabbit reposes on the sill.
It contemplates its yellow interiors of wish. How I sit on my nest.

Of this you may rest assured. Insured. My next
act will be politic. My next act will be brie

and chardonnay. Petite sirah, sirrah. Not salt
and teabags, little paper trysts

but a pigeon's plash of feathers as dusk falls at the spring.
As the spring folds in its witness, draws its beasts.

He reached right up and caught the bird. Held its terror
bodied in his palm. Nevermind that he would let it go.

In a moment. For a moment. Could not drink.

3.

So turn from me a timber, like a workglove, like a bride
like the quick snap of the last chalk in the box.

Roll from me like a blood orange, like a goddamn string of pearls.
Fizz to tissue like a cheap corsage.

4.

Listen, the woman says, *relinquish everything.*
In her cup, the grounds have settled.

>   (The grass in April trammeled and still white
>   and the mountains neither black nor blue,
>   nor green, nor made of smoke—)

In the kitchen there are cardamom and bacon grease and pears
and mail arriving in its envelope.

5.

Snip off your morning snags of hair, gather the bitten half-moons of your nails.

>   Concede this as you would a prayer, a point
>
>   in your enemy's debate:
>
>   As if you could believe it, but do not.
>
>   That rain unlocked its pilgrimage.
>
>   That loosestrife spread through the swamp.
>
>   Mermaid's purses. Cuttlefish. What is given up.
>
>   The bricks of the piazza and the shine.

Shatter and Thrust As a Series of Silver Gelatin Prints

If the birches' sticks are edged in black, then silence
means consent. If a skiff slips loose

from its mooring, then nothing can be tied
to a bed or elsewhere, no one can be held

though the white lake in the distance still craves the diver's form
remembering how muscular, how slim,

and how its water, spring-fed, cold, curled
around his body as he dove—

If the mirror in her room could play it back, scene by scene, across its silver skin,
each moment as it was, its arc and gleam,

then the secret language that precedes desire
could be deciphered, spoken in, annulled.

Instead she writes *oh fuck oh fuck*, the f's
curling back on themselves, the way she's been taught to, scene by scene

as the boy in the memory lights a spliff, hand cupped,
in no distress, not looking up. Then the little bobbin shuttles left

still spooling out its thread, as if to speak, as if to draw him back
though lately she thinks it is more

that a thin communion snaps in two each morning as she wakes   (Don't tell
us about the heart you beg Tell us about the flesh Because everyone speaks

in the offing Everyone's broken inside Always already &c.,) But see:
if grass slants dark in the snow-field, if a bird flew

watching for snares, if the bird were a sparrow launched in a reckless wind,
if she felt herself entangled, if she could not close her wing,

then extricated, fitted with a band—
If opening the hand would give release

—a seamless gesture, flight and opening—
then the body might give up its wish, relinquish

what it is: a white field of desire, a field of questions asking
toward their end. If I say *make it hurt* if I say *get the belt*

I am thinking of the freeway, its plastic barricades,
and of such little solace as there is. The boy in oval sunglasses

squatting in the dust, his look intent; the boy splayed on the bed
asleep or half asleep, her coming in—

The photographs she's taken in her mind
because the body can't be trusted, because the body

soon forgets, though absence enters, claims her
as its own. If a stopsign slants through the morning facing the other way,

if the post is splintered, the grain of it rough in the print
on this road I walk down toward my end

the white erasure hovering, its dream of being found
and mine, of brokenness beyond repair—

beyond want of repair—then the rowboats, too,
are errant, slipping past the buoys. How well I loved you in that other place

I once called *home*, I once called *manifest*.
As if all that burned were burning. In that room where the light cried out.

How small the body seems now. How tough, how absolute.
When I say *hurt me*, this is what I mean.

Self Portrait as Dido

extremum hoc miserae det munus amanti:
tempus inane peto . . .
dum mea me uictam doceat fortuna dolere.
                     The Aeneid, *Book IV*

She has come at last to a flickering place
    where sun swirls on the rockface by the spring
moving its blue and yellow hands
    then vanishing, adept, adept
The way desire passes her
    over now, aloof, or splinters
through the pines along the road,
    the quick stripes in succession
flailing her as she drives, the voice
    on the cellphone audible, then not,

then audible again. As when, in the studio,
    the teacher instructs her to hold
two things in the body: extension
    and retraction: one part of the thigh
drawn in, the other
    turning out. How the grain
of the muscle moves
    like the pull of *ask*
and *answer*, a pain she will not flinch from
    as she focuses her gaze
on the variegated woodstripe of the floor.

As, under the flicker, granite, slate. Clank
        of her boots in the streambed, last year's grizzled
needles on the rocks. She has come at last
        to a drop-off, a space too sheer
to cross: how to live with the flicker
        touching her face but not. The never-touching,
never-coming-to. Must she unravel what she knows she knows
        as the water, raveling outward
shrinks in the pool each day, till the light
        can barely reach it, will not, can't? Because things

        renounce each other (she tells
herself) a little more each day: As affection
        leaves the body, as sun comes late to the screen,
while the spring moves back, moves back
        from what it loves.

        Cicadas throb in the distance
as defiance, in a corner of her mind
        flares up from its sand-bed, from the place
she banked and left it, tried
        to leave. She holds it in her being
as a word, unspoken, hovers in the mouth.
        As the gaze holds back its hunger, as a thief
holds back intent. If only
        there were violence to steer
her body toward (she turns it
        like a smooth stone in her thought), a scrap

of paper scrawled *come naked and alone*
        to make of sorrow some exquisite thing.
How long will it take, she wonders
        this rending, stitch by stitch? She turns
her face to the half-light where branches
        cast their net across her hands.

Night in the Formal Garden

Black lilies on black water. Where inky
tendrils coil into ink. Is it night

that you recall, or night we've fallen into?

As many months without you now
as with.

A red light in black water.

And the single body lathes in sleep
its tangled manufactury of dream.

The body alive to its impulse, trying to crush it.

Again. Again. Again. Again.

Red light in black water.

As if it could renounce both noun and verb

for a black street in the city where deer are seen to cross.

The sign that indicates.

As if between *curb* and *wood*
there could be truce.

What use to say, *I remember*—

What use begin, *I dreamed the weeks*

were like a yellow thicket, broken back?

You don't believe in ritual. Nor I
in consolation.

Red paper on black water.

What would be sodden
if I picked it up.

How, seeing none, the body

cleaves against its form. It wills a force
to hold it

down, crush out the light,

tear out its silken wish.

But none arrives to break it.

The weeks grown up like garrisons, like law.

White snow on black water.

Forgive the body her insistent prayer—

In Absentia

to my body

*

a page

new snow

blankety-

      blank

a rancid year

thrown out

an old house clean

dear body

      where

are you living now

myself herein

what house I can construct

      such roof

      as I can manage

whatever walls

as I can now arrange

dear body

give no quarter

      dear body

write when you can

my address tent

in treason   tree sun   help

to winter me a small belief

since knowing you

                   were finest

            though I miss—

*

sky on sky of snow-light

field on field of snow

white amnesty

                   white alcatraz

I am thinking even now

of things we spoke of months ago

dear envelope   dear gesture

dear lucky ticket wind-flicked down the street

to be as you   all pinnace   and all unruly hair

all birdcage   all remittance

all secrecy turned rightside like a coat

to be both slip and breakage

bright robbery   bright rogue

I cannot solve you   x

does not appear

*

witness me

dear figment

a stolen archery

       harmatia

the one flaw in the cup

the one   sure thing

I hit and miss

       the mark

         your mark

   wherein I'm done

     undone

*

dear prodigal   who

do you sleep with

when you are awake

in all your holy

and unholy holes

who takes you   where

do they take you

each astonished afternoon

whose passages

      do you traverse

whose hand   on your chest

what data   in the body's hot machine

*

what then must I relinquish

what small relentless prayer

half moth   half angel   beats its raggy wing

against the window   crazed with rain

dear resident   can you forgive

the ardent thing I am

all errancy   all ache   all botched attempt

forgive my klutzy presence   my sweet

futility   I will not give you up

can make no truce

*

dear body   you do not reply

days pass   white on white

the snow

drifts back

and forth   relentless thing

my little tent   does not provide

      is neither here nor there

         dear vestibule

in which I could be   was

I know you have your reasons

but still   there are a few things I should say

dear handshake   you were splendid

dear torso   I   could not have asked for more

dear sternum   thanks for trying

I'm sure you did your best

and you   poor ribcage

do you break

or breathe

*

winter me believer

an armory of snow

field on field   indrifted

indrifted   door on door

where sorrow-birds

sit huddled   that it was once

aflame   this figure

made for bearing

cannot bear

*

dear duncecap   I cannot believe

you still will not reply

I render   all I am   apology

dear body   are you busy

dear body   cut me some slack

it's true I am encamped

in forest dark with pine

it's true I forage what relief I can

but I still have a fire   a little sustenance

and also   need but little

a cup   a small belief

dear body   send a letter

make it *a*

*

dear unraveled angel   say

you will return   brazen

in your flesh   your restless hair

my scavenger apostle   my bright

impenitent   dear incident

dear mooncalf   say you'll touch   re-

member   blaze   my way

*

then sleep dear body   lionhearted sleep

in each small twig a sign   you still abide

but here is only snow   too deep to pass

silence plied with silence   white with white

you who left me   promised

that you would not return

                           & you do not

what could be   was

though you & I   are lost

       dear shipwreck

            piece by piece

      in silence   hold   as ever   fast

      each   to what we still   must be

                 after a fashion   true

CLOISTER

day after day   of winter
day after day   at the brink
of freezing   breaking open

throwing my body away—

*

cloud blaze over field
of stubblecorn and slate

stones give way beneath me
a thin nest drops from the tree

if grief too is a form of prayer
then I am most devout

sorrow without end   amen   amen

*

my summer clothes   white gauzes   put away

*

your image   not discernable
in reliquary light   I pray   I pray
but you are mute   as god

*

my novena   *please return*
each white mouth   of nine   full moons
here now   on the tenth month
you do not

*

although I pray   impossible
my vow is poverty   I claim
no house   no address   no remorse

*

how winter pinks the morning light
I wake to sun   mere slippage
through the trees   the prayer my body prays
each morning does not change
I wash my face   my hands   my eyes
I cannot change   my prayer

*

in the grey light of a morning
my 37th year   today   my birth-
day   tinged with snow   I could
have a date with concrete
why not   plunge
so finely
no regret

*

you absence furled   as sky
informs me   not   to grieve
how I mistook   the body
for the breath

*

though I am dim   novitiate   my same
rebellious heart   wants   (not allowable)
not to perish   I can be
no cool marble   angel   I will burn

*

I do know what you're thinking dear
but I am not an insect
unbalanced by the light   not a moth

gone spiraling   toward flame
I am a bird on fire   winging   through the dark
my small song   *break me, break me*
finally, once   and for all

RANSOM

As if in simple ransack, gin-light
snapping backwards in the sky.
A thrashing. As of branches. As
of hands. The rest was pitch and scatter.
The year, a flicker of birds. A film
of sparrows preening, taking off.

Then, desire in the inmost room.
A blooming, as of salt-stain.
As of wound. How the seam
burst from its stitches. Pollen
in the girded, girdled air.

Awash between sunder and edgeless
don't tell them what was fastened
in my eye. An instinct
to be broken. A vacancy
wound brightly on the spool.

STYE

Look how the morsel sets itself, stiff red rocklet risen
at night as from the sea. What scald creeps from the thermal vent

to swell the narrow seam, what vision that the body
will not take. If I poultice it with salt, with tea, with some

bright herb, if I rub it with a gold ring will it break
open, finally. If I pierce it with a pin. Will all the tears

or stares come out. Will all the tyrant angers of my eye. Because
I must not dream of you, I learn to rummage off

the tiny cups and saucers in my blood. But admit defeat
and defiance grows another limb: this leather pouch that hardens

will not slough. How obstinate desire is
to house my raffled light, to spider on the eye's persistent stalk. Seal up

my rife inflection. Detain me cell by cell. Poor blunderer who cannot forge
even a slim resistance, a glimpse, a human frame.

In Motion

Alone on Sunday afternoon, I watch the dog's paws twitching as he sleeps.
His dream turns like a newsreel, simple chase
between snapped branches, lurching toward a sky,
the path irrelevant, his prey a prayer, the blue flame of his being
flared to high. Call it *small recurrent animal,* this dream
that all dogs dream, like that relentless dream of ropes and stays
in which I turn my body like a filmstrip
to the light. Yes, pin me
to the window, watch me jerk
from frame to animated frame. Each small, belabored increment. Each day
a pink sun moving south against the wall
glides through the strictures of winter. The camera
lucida or obscure. Here are my lumpy socks, my unmade bed. No tragedy
in these particulars. But friends, when I sit at your table
there's a voice in me that says *Give*
up. Give up. It pumps along like a half-dead frog.
Ladies and gentlemen, it says, *this train has left the station. Wave*
to your friends on the platform. You may begin
to panic at any time.

This Hope

Whole tilt-a-whirls of leafshow, snow. And now
the burgeoning trees. The brittle seasons raise their lights

as slight green grassblade
pokes from last year's rusk. Elsewhere,

you tell me I should have a heart
swollen with the vigor of this scene,

but I still hold these feathers in my hands.
I thought I was a bird. I am no bird.

Here, the hangdog streetlamp. There, the dastard sky.
What bed shall I assemble? Nest in the drainpipe, sticky box,

dirty blankets tangled in the park. No one loves
the rancid, the bereft. Nothing in me

maddens, I assure, but all this rankled could-be
will not hush. Itinerant, I lionize, I ravage

toward despair. I push the edge until I've mangled
every beautiful thing. Now I'll put on makeup,

zip up my dress of mirrors. Each will show
your laughing mouth, will tilt your smile back. Because I cannot

stand myself. Because I toss and turn
in my bones like a fraudulent angel. And what a pesky

arrogance, this hope. Call me monster, monstrance, call me
off. Spring's a lovely season after all,

every garish leaf lit from within. My sweet
amnesiac scholar, I realize that you wish me

some repose. Hold me. Drink me
from this cup. Whisper in my ear,

Between us there must be no tenderness.
Then pin in my arm behind my back. Do it. Make it

hurt. I'll cry uncle for you, I'll cry anything.
Just thrash me till I can't recall

what it was I wanted. Bliss, whatever
you ask for. Sin me. Sin me again.

DETACHMENT

Hold me, stranger. Press me close
in the pearly morning light. I will dream us coffee,
the paper, pears. These I have wanted, asked for,
had. But all things pass away. How often in this life
does someone say, *Forgive me?* You half-asleep and tender
in my bed. I will make a small account of love, I will count on the stumps
    of my fingers
all the things I have clung to: blankets, bedframes, tufts of hair,
an old red pickup truck, a shell glossed dull with river mud, a shirt,
    a piece of fruit—
Whatever fades or fails me. I am as close now to disaster
as I have ever been. Help me assume, dear stranger,
a modest setting-forth. No art, no
savage hope. Last night you put your hands
around my neck. Tell me this was beautiful.
Say we wake unscathed. Fold
your arms around me now. Tell me
there are things that can be kept.

HARMONIC

You have a beautiful spine, he said, admiring her bones:
how the body drops from its axis into a string of vowels,
every chakra a station emitting its one desire, its singular
harmonic, its whirlwind in the mouth, the mouth a red umbrella
and the way the ribs snap tight. Say yes
to the body's sweetness. *Yes.* As if from my brilliant
exile, that mudflare, sun, that silver raft of flame, there might yet be
some word could call me home. Say she. Say me. What matters:
there was in fact an hour broken clean
before he whispered, *Darling, I'm sorry, I have to go,*
before they walked together snagged in a brief embrace,
the wind curled in her collar, a chill in her thin blue coat, when there their limbs
were a small remittance, a small astonishment, the slow vowel
and the reverb, what wintered in them taking its ease in the corner.

What to Ask for, How to See

1. *Those Are Pearls*

Say the eye is a tidepool. Allow, within it, an unfolding
blue.
      "The error is not to fall, but to fall
                from no height."

The thin bird sees the vestige. Where I grappled
through the night. He would not answer
the question. Although I asked and asked. And the feather

was an accident. No sign.

2. *Eat Me When I'm Bigger* (with a quote from *Walden*)

Could call the body
shelter: Bolts in the softwood. Each instinctive turn. Scratchings
moused in the cupboard. A flimsy foothold, flimsy
holding-in.

      How each alarmed entrance
                proves the span. What shadows me:

the floater in my eye, this knot that shelters, troll-like
beneath my shoulder bone—

                my greatest skill has been to want but little

emits a restless presence on the stair.

3. *Float Like a Butterfly, Sting*

Let's go still further. Carry me to bed.

As when, a child, I'd pretend to sleep
cold in the backseat, star-enclosed
to feel my father hoist me to his chest.

But if prayer

is a useless flailing, teach me
how to fight. Hit me where the organs hunker
down behind the flesh. What clumps

along on the inside must not
stay unhurt. My capsized
invitation. Unruly height or heist.

The larva in the attic
held by a net of threads.

WHAT SHE SEES WHEN SHE HUSHES
from Gertrude Stein

i.

at any time
        it rains
and if it rains
      no fruit
the wild grasses
        even if
and therefore

ii.

If it rains her name is often.
"There are no—is no need."

To work very hard in a garden
although she is exhausted.

"The green things have black roots
& the black roots have red stems."

When grass is cut it does not matter
(again and again the sky)

How often after careful
attention she refused.

So to speak was not allowed completely.

iii

often if it rains
the grass is dark
she shuts her eyes

she is very careful
then to throw it away

the grasses
he cannot caress
and it is very small

what adding means

iv.

(if it rains
it does not matter

the way in which
she does not grow

"green things
have black roots

& black roots
have red stems"

all the birds
are not afraid

then when she
shuts her eyes)

v.

So to speak was not allowed completely.
Something comes and then it follows them.
"It has been very troublesome"

to work very hard in a garden
though once in a while it rains
a day is not really a day

"No one has left anyone"

Awake once every morning
she grows tomatoes and roses and pinks
(there seems to be so much need)

and she is very careful
then to throw it away
words as well as things and distribution.

AND AFTER

Caught in the oak tree's wickering light, knee-deep,
without rescue, I have grown raw white as a mollusk. I can't bear

to hear music, no longer listen to the radio. In this town
there are toxic salt-flats, lemon trees, the smell of lanolin.

In the streets there are cathedrals, marble forms of saints. The saint
with a wasp in his mouth, saint with a rabbit

hedged beneath his arm. Behind the rabbit's eye, a coiled spring.
But my hands, a tattered ledger, offer only evidence

without imperative. I found a nest of bees inside the grill
and lit them each on fire, rubbed their soot and honey in my hair.

But there was no visitation, no vision that could lend me back the day.
The rabbit squirmed from the stone grasp of the saint. Already, friend,
    I murmured, I like you

more than is meet. I will bring you blood and muslin, annoint your lips
with milk, tie you by the leg to the mulberry tree.

I will drop ink on your tongue to be sure you speak no ill
till the workmen come with leather on their hands. I know one bit of magic:

how to turn invisible in a room. The trick
is turning visible again. I will make a clipped beginning

but I say again I am no kind of bird. In this town there are roofs
of copper, angelica staves in the yard. In this language

the word for *lid* is the same as the word for *sky*.

[GHOST RIVER]

another rampant summer   scorches on its track
past dumpstered alleys   lanky truant trees

steam from the power plant rises   my cataracted eye
as weather's blue contingent   flanks

the either   / or
can just make out   the river   glinting

through the leaves   a marriage ticking   stitch by stitch
must not allow   the minute

inhabit small   remote
place of abdication   proceed at measured pace

through ordinary city streets   where spendthrift
thistle burgeons in the lot

    hot asphalt   call it blacktop   invents a brief
    mirage   between us   no more speaking

        so too the body   flickers back

[PURGATORIO]

wind through the ash tree, thrashing
admits a clumsy syntax

as when his dirty fingers last
risked, then grasped
my hair

      frisk back the sheet of air
         (*do, do*)

wind was black, night silver
with itself.

in sleep we gather up
our limbs   a similar alone

I realize now I wanted
the hurt sky   thrown asunder

then all my hungers opened on their hinge

[BONE IN, BONE OUT]

how gaunt the wires are   the air   I once believed
whatever cries the tawny birds emit

that something held us   god of lipstick   god of sticky notes
now I scale the trestle   its spine of rotten wood

to tag the rusty angles with my name
with something   sign   or pictograph

o god of black electric lines   lord of high-speed trains

if I lift up   my skirt for you beneath the overpass   if I
kneel down and let you fill   my mouth

will you touch me   where I cannot reach   admit
me to myself   I promise I'll stop popping off

the heads of baby rabbits   little silky mice   and other
restless creatures   that scuffle in the walls   shells of peas

in the pea-pan   yards and yards of wool I'll never knit

[POSTINDUSTRIAL / ORPHEUS]

buckthorn grates the gulfstream   into wimpy curls
    as rabbits flee along the access road   but I'm far beyond
the cyclone fence   have left my compact car

    I don't know when the footage   cut to black and white
only the grim horizon   the field in low-res flicker as I walk
    the hard-stemmed winter grasses   crackle at my waist   love,

what a lie belief is   soil here for every weedy thing
    as each white rootlet needles in   spreads its livid hair
spiny plants whose names   I do not know

    only the colder hours   distinguish day from night
I lie along the ground   but do not sleep   recall a kitchen table
    squid ink pasta   yellow apples   cake   how easily a life

drops from its peg   at times I see an old   wrecked plane
    mangled in its shelter by an oak   the leaves and I   are silver
wave   our hands   at times a narrow visage   flickers in the bark

    the face a man's   I do not recognize
still have my same old leather bag   my pad   and pencil stub
    I hope you will forgive me   for all

I could not see   although I bartered   with what little art—

DIDO IN WINTER

Dear all-purpose match head:
I saw your blue corona, struck

flare up. Briefly,
briefly, two arched wings of flame.

These days they say
I'm inconsolable. My small

acts of defiance break
like sticks.

If I could receive
a letter, feel at least

the scrape: your mind against
my curiosity.

How much I miss
our bodies. Mine

gone limping off
to god-knows-where.

It's frozen now. The air,
the yellow mud

too hard to yield to a shovel.
Dear once-was, do you hear?

I can survive the damn insipid sky
but not the way I smolder, cigarette

pressed to skin, inward
to a figment of myself.

A 16MM FILM (IN BLACK & WHITE)

Shapes of birds on the river. Slight backscatter of snow.

The water moves and moves in the injured light.

How to impress upon you. You, or anyone

this phase, this apprehension, this slope down to the shore.

Sun through a window smeared with grime. Where is the future I could

pretend myself into? Whatever it was you asked for

this is what you get: Hanks of salt grass, grainy rock,

silver wash of light along the bridge.

A hand grips rebar, the window breaks, then it all goes black.

Someone sobbing in another room—

This isn't the end of the movie.

River, the shapes of birds.

My voice is a pile I pick through.

The body won't disperse.

Must I consent to this day or the next?

DIDO TO THE LITTLE MATCHGIRL

Barefoot in the snow, you're a specialist
in pathos, I can see. Even at six you have a knack for it.
But take my word for it, honey: You can't just sit there freezing
by the wall. I know how it is to want things,
to tie yourself to the bed because it burns. I can see you're *that* kind of girl
dreaming of a lavish room and cake. But let me tell you something:
     you can be queen
of the airwaves and still the signal's weak. Don't like
yourself too much. I used to believe two bodies
could cross out each other's grief, that a girl
could take some comfort for herself. But once it starts, a heart will not stop
breaking, that's the thing. I'll tell you how it's going to be:
go with the man in the car. When he asks if you're a pervert
nod and tell him yes. You don't have to know what the word means. Just
do what he wants. Because the more you practice giving up
the readier you'll be. You won't be twirling in a dress
singing, *make me a match*. Build yourself a bedroom, a house
of straw and thatch. Just strike one, then another. You dirty
little bitch. Because the place for a girl like you
is not on the common street. The place
for a woman who burns is in the fire.

Contrivance (Matchgirl's Reply)

Make a new alliance. Sentences. No body.
Head and hands.

It's not enough
to be a girl

I have to be good at it too?

And day by day I fail so beautifully.

My tongue: imprudent
instrument. My mouth: discrepant gloss.

A morning's tattered light and a trick for saying never.

A body wants to be itself. Ridiculous contraption.

Each small sip of air and light through the various rooms—

Heart, we will not speak of you again.

PRAYER

Bathrooms are the best locale.
All that waste and water and getting clean.

Or trains. The nearly equal passengers.

A phone rings in the kitchen but no one picks it up.
Milk goes bad at room temp. You don't check your email anymore.

Could only scrawl a message: "I _____ you
with all my harm." Each day stacked in the sideboard. Folded, white—

Why can't I snap the wishbone, learn to tolerate the chilly floors?

If breath by breath I reckon, if I am to approximate myself—

(*This*, then *that*, then *this* again. Stutter, step, a step.)

Like that woman in the corner seat. I can't tell if she's sleeping
or in pain.

If you won't, then count my leavings.

Bright amnesiac instance,
little red thread on my jeans.

Thread

It's important these days to practice having nothing
to say. Hours accrue, the white amnesia of work. What else is prayer if not a place
a body can burn itself up in? Offal, joss, a bit of chalky clay. The wish my body
    used to be.
Contingent of unanswered, it whimpers now, it barely

Nevermind. I wake up in a leaky house, the window in my study iced
this far into winter and still as yet no sign. Triangulated gesture: trying, praying,
giving up. Yank of another morning, but nothing breaks me
hard enough. The winter garden limping through its phase, the lemon balm
    unfurling

from its pot. When I walk across the street now, I'm crossing
    without confidence
or hope. Do you need them to move forward. Yet I'm true to my asking.
    My tsking. I shuffle
the tarot deck but the same few cards emerge. Dear Kate, I am still suspicious
    of solace
but I try to drink enough water to avoid persistent thirst. It was a place
    to call home

and we called it that. I miss the pale light on the houses. Not quite everything
    was lost,
but the best things won't come back. I don't know what anyone does in the face
    of this.
People say they *have to believe* that *something good will happen*. That isn't belief,
it's a precept, it's a survival skill. In the story the Zen master told, I am

the unenlightened man. Could there be a difference. Could there be a place
to bed down. These days, the winter garden wilts behind its plastic tarp.
    Shadows of birds
on the houses, seedling slips of green. I can't say what will make it
    and what won't.
Goodbye, little everything, and thanks for trying to try. *If* is a very tiny word

to hold in one's defense. They say it's the fight in the dog that counts;
it isn't the dog in the fight.

LETTER TO ELIZABETH BISHOP

December 24th, upon re-reading "Don't Kill Yourself."

Forgive me if I'm too familiar.
We're not used to letters anymore
(the kind in ink, one's own hand on a page)
and I know you're a private person. Still,
no one's here except the dog and me
and the light on the windows is precisely pink,
a color you would have loved
had you been here to see it. You might have appreciated, too, the light noise
of the cars, even perhaps the splotchy snow
in the park across the road. Winter that won't stay,
won't go, can't quite establish itself

as some things do. But I digress. Dear Elizabeth:
This morning I woke too early
and watched out of the corner of my eye
a grey mouse trouble the floor, back and forth, back
and forth, first one side then the other, dashing—no, gliding really,
    from the dog dish
to the stove. My habits, though, are not
so regular. And you? I think you must
have been an early riser. Would you

have watched the mouse and let it be,
its thievery, its tiny wants, its odd,
impudent presence in the house? There are these losses
that I just can't master. But here you are, all cool
formality, your cities crashing down with delicate rage.
"In the meantime you go on your way
vertical, melancholy." Tell me again

about the armadillo, the squashing fire balloons, the loves that left us
and will not come back. "A racket of which nobody
knows the why or wherefore." My friend,
I must confide: I burn too hot. Show me metallic
moonlight, cold imploding lichen on the rocks.
You said it best when you said
there's an element bearable to no mortal.
It's all I am and might be, and am not.

Raveling

This winter I learn to knit: a green and purple scarf,
which could be my last undoing, this *casting on*
and *binding off*, a way to connect

each moment to the next. It's a swaddling
operation for a mind that can't be stilled. Because we are no longer
real to one another, this winter I walk on snow crust

gone vitreous with cold, shadows on it
lavender, green ice on the pond. A plastic sheet that shreds
and shreds in wind. At times, this park

looks beautiful, but I'm a stranger in it.
Only phrases keep me: *made
of sterner stuff*, they say. They say *aloof* or *politic* or

soon when the weather breaks. The thornbush faintly
red now, and two unyielding greys: green-grey branches
pinioned on grey sky. The snow is a constant

burning, and my body—slow, molecular—also a kind of fire
almost, they say, *unstoppable.* When did it come
to this. I hear myself say *harbor me*

although there is no harbor I can see
no one else to speak to,
and the trail breaks off

to *every possible willow.* Around me, ice crust circles
with an insane gleam and glare
that holds me, then gives way beneath my boot. The sky

in its abstract sphere, unfurls. Today I have to practice
how to breathe. Memory's insistent,
too dangerous to touch. Each small amnesia

till I ghost myself.

On the Obsolescence of Prayer

Because my mouth is a twin embarrassment: 1) the shape
of my wiry lips, and 2) my crooked teeth. Then 3) this tongue

that limps and snags on speech. I mean, it speaks
but does not speak me well. Today it's a different color—

black would be hyperbolic, so let's call it
indigo. Let's call it *mouse with strychnine,* let's call it

archipeligo of doubt. Because *blue has no dimensions
it is beyond dimension.* And when I said Despair

had its foot on my neck, did you think I meant my suffering
was allegorical? What I mean is that I trust you

but maybe not enough. And if you gave me a field of daffodils,
I'd gouge out both my eyes. You see? Because, as the gynecologist

said, *Your cervix today looks friable,* and I thought, *Like a steak?
Be sure to see your PCP,* and I thought, *I don't do drugs*

but on second thought, it seems like a good idea. There's a lot to be said
for prevention, for staying a little starved. Because all I've ever wanted

is a tattoo of myself all over myself, only thinner—
or maybe, failing that, someplace quiet and warm. You see, I'm lost in a forest

I dreamed up on my own. All night I've listened to the leaves' applause, the gossip
of the live-oak, the jack pine stitching its shroud. Mosquitoes

lisp in the underbrush, perched and waiting to feed, or fat, already rubied
with my blood. I smash them against my arms, I smear them

on my thigh. In this I take satisfaction. Sometimes, I let them bite me
and then just fly away. Something may as well be bred

and they can't help the fact. I mean I am encamped, pitched
in the far dark field. It's a place not even you can reach.

Because every day I wake behind my own unbeautiful face
in this ruined amphitheater where I pray. I mean, I play

at making house alone. My small voice doesn't carry far
beyond the sharp-edged grass. I know God hears,

but won't reply. This is something
but it isn't love. If I could,

I'd send you a sparrow, a message strapped
to her wing. *Find me. Answer this letter, if you can.*

Afternoon Traffic and Weather

The strong man who bent quarters with his teeth

until age one hundred and five

was struck and killed by a mini-van today

and the dog will not stop growling

at the shadows of birds on the house next door

blown-out shapes on siding, black on green—

There are two types of houses: those on which the birds

cast shadows, and those on which they don't. I'm the first kind of house

but you knew that already. How, driving to work I mistook

a bumper sticker ("safety is my goal") for one that read "no beauty

is in my soul." Goddamn these happy people

and their television sets. I beg them to stop *The Shining*

but I just can't look away. Dear metal barricade, dear rack

of lamb. Forgive me. The nasty thing I said

was nothing compared with what I meant to say. Because *one day at a time*

is a trick for saying never. And I still don't understand

where I made the first mistake

but it must've been a dusie. I thought I was beautiful

all this time. I thought I could make a go. When I stood stock still

in the crosswalk, in my head it all made sense.

V.

FORAGE

Permit a clamped horizon, a peach tree's puny fruit.

Because when you asked my name, I startled back
into my skin. The blot on my nib an inkling. Our bodies snagged in the trace

of all our prior movements as if in a bolt of cloth, a ball of string. So motion
is a textile art. I thought I had to circle back, thereby undo my steps. But press

or disassemble,
some things keep wanting to be. The burl

of your hair, for instance: this yolk and caul
that winter in an egg.

And the migratory light that banks along the wall
could be called insistence

if this story of a body
would not be divvied, would not be denied.

Don't name it harbor, thrush, or breath. My faulty understanding
reconnoitered by the wind.

At Horseneck, the galloping ocean sweeps me out.

APOLOGIA

How I order my intention. Now

permit, dismiss. The curtain
swagged
against its frame

as the incandescent goldfish
spreads its shared relation through the room.

My love, forgive the archival trees.

That they hoard
their botched
transcription   (of sunlight

into space),   that the elm transmits
its errancy

along the performative
drive. Forgive

the pore
its opening,
that errand

into dirt;
the porcelain

occlusion of the egg. We must not crack

our egg tooth. Yet the angry
floor wants swept. I think

there must be water
the cables cannot span

And I can no longer hold
myself

palmwise, chaffed to the wind.

HIKE

Trip from the valley, upward. A path I could traverse. Waste of high rock,
    unseasonable cold.

The field, a green admittance. White phlox spread on rockface sharp
    as wings. There is

no form of binding. Swerve through the long chicane. Some animal, ancestral
    or extinct.
What kind of animal

must I be. I will consult the map. Intransitive, I snow
    or sleep. I falter where the gradient permits.

My bearing is approximate. The air distills a lake.
    I want I cannot calculate the span. What pack

should I have carried? Splay out my gear on rocks.

What kind of reluctance. The surface pockmarked, varying in hue.

BEATIFICATION

There were hyacinths warm as waffles, & starvation seemed just

like a dream, silvery and elegant
as the apple blossoms churning out their suds

in the small groves on the hillsides. Because the moon

was a lavender saltlick & because, when I opened
my mouth, a girl-ghost flickered right

out of my throat. Then I walked through the streets
as a penitent, begging you for a word. Then I climbed the 100 basilica steps

on my knees. Then I lit 1000 votives
and wept 1,000,000,000 tears. I begged for a god

who could hear me. I annealed myself in prayer. Still, you pressed your hands
to my lips till I wasn't real. Outside there was mud & crocuses

sprang up like purple speakers from the loam. Deafening frog song pumped
from tiny, unseen frogs. There were little lame balloon men

afoot in every square, trolling
for dates in every city park. How they wheeled their tanks

past the fountains. How they twisted balloons into shapes. Rocketships
    and monkeys.
Skyscrapers and giraffes. Then the streets unfurled a renaissance of bikes.

You don't even know which questions.

You don't even know
which words.

I wanted your voice
to be in me. I wanted the dirt on your hands.

Because the grass was green as instinct & algae swarmed through the pond
like a diver's hair, like the Horseshoe Nebula.

Now, it's spring on the carnival rides. On the buildings, banners saying *do, do, do.*

Next time, we'll be strangers
but I swear, I'll know who you are. I promise

I'll be the three-headed dog, all slobber, all rolling tongue. I promise
I'll be the boatman. Look: I can swim the length of the pool in a single breath.

When I fell asleep on a park bench, sunlight filled my veins.
Now I am "illumined." My skin is a radiant isotope.

My lungs are a sea wasp, pulsing under glass.

Airplane Poem

disjunctive interval   new wood floors
salt flats span the desert   rusty white
as thieves   there are objects I'd like

to abandon   stray dishes   hazy mirrors
but all my problems are problems
of distance vs. time   so my blizzards grow enormous

against sweet little girls   their scratchy party dresses
chafe my thighs   uncharitable airspace thoughts
her appaloosa legs   and friend in the olympiad

of crying babies   yours   would be the best
even the wakeful babies   little predators
wait in the grayscale with their hazel eyes

but each time I vow to be different
I become more like myself   an almond
or a lone pistachio   where grains of coffee

constellate the sink   wherever it was we were
resplendent populace   the hives began
to glisten   honey drooped

from the seam   I watched my body drink you
on the train we were pressed forward
into the darker angles of ourselves

tiny stilt lines splinter out   across
the plexiglass   every hour on the hour
what can be possible now

Switch

When lights flipped on and off through the city, this was the morse code

of your never-coming-back. The billboards knew it,

also the art museum. The flutter of the switches being

a kind of unnamed performance, a kind of inaccurate approximation

of the phrase *whatever you want.* I thought then of the sailor

who set off in the glass-bottomed ship

of her grief, only to find the island already inhabited. It's a familiar story.

It's true there were descriptions of the city

to offset the protagonist's despair, the violence justifiable

when studied a second time. The screech of tires seemed then

like some sort of new beginning. I opened the valves

of my body and prayed for rain.

APOLOGIA

Dear reader: here's where I'm standing: stage left
in the darkness, lured by a spotlit shaft. The bulb pushes down
like an ego. The bulb is in fact an ego. Who could parse it, pass it,

stand beneath its silver cone of light? But see me, operatic
in my pearls? My taffeta, my gloves and tortise-shell. I'm clearing
my throat for an aria, I am about to speak. (Notice

I said *glove* and not the other word. There are words allowed
in poems, there are words that must be excised.) And I'll tell you
a story about that. Remember the guy last night? It hurt

but I couldn't say so, the cat had stolen my breath. I woke up sore
but not enough. And, morning-bruised, I don't regret a thing.
Because this is what I am choosing. Because I am so tired anyway

of wishing for your hands, for your fierce and careful body, your teasing
and bad teeth. But you green fire, almond tree, you (may I call you *you*?)
who said, *it has to be like this,*

who pastured me a day, take my best, my finest hope,
and break it. I'm throwing all this memory away
because what good does it do to photograph a thing? Photos give the look of it,
    that's all.

Sorry reader, that wasn't you. I was having a moment.

The question we are all asking, I wrote in my little book, *is how the poem, given
its origin in emotion, given its problem of longing, can exist at the present time.*

The question is how and whether I can continue to exist.

So I don't know what to tell you now, how to position my mouth
around what I can't stand and don't want to: the lack of hands, the lack of words,
the lack of a flattering light, the words and the wanting to speak them,
    the stutter shot

through the body, the terrible wanting to be. Don't you see
how I've prayed to the chickens
ever since I ate them in a hotdog at the beach? The flavor

was portobello, but what does a flavor *do*? Dear chickens, should I apologize
for loving you imperfectly, or at all? Forgive me
for my not-knockwurst, for this hole in my skin where the pleasure goes.

And how I am all frilly-like, thwacked in my tiny frame.
Is you afraid you break me sweetums
like you say you is? Forgive I don't do dancerly with table top and booze

but people say to be myself
and then they say I'm wrong. Forgive me for my wayward
parts. They are so bent and true. They are so non-detachable.
    They are so boohoohoo.

I fear I have no blueprint and no tumescent hope. Please.
Take this poem anyway. Take this body. Let its holes intrude.

Outage

Look at me loving you, figment and all.

Forgive me for this mouth that says *I want.*

For this body, its entreaty. Rope and ocean. Ocean, rope.

As a child I was taught *O is for obstinate.*

Little Miss O, so stubborn. No more of your knocking, imploring,
    your sobbing. Go to your room.

But I need to be this shadow through the summer leaves, I need
    to be inconsolable

for as long as this takes. Neighbor, please stop

with the circular saw. It gives incessant headache

while I'm trying to wrap my brain around a fact. Like a toy boat bobbing

in a flooded basement, what I need is less reality, fewer uplifting sayings.

Fuck *acceptance.* Fuck you, *letting go.* I'll surrender into the moment

when the moment starts to live up to its name. Meanwhile, I mean to cultivate

a backyard full of sisal and avocado trees. I mean

I need to hold this hope in my hands till it falls apart.

When you flip the switch, the power comes back on.

LAUNCH
for Falcon Heene

I did not mean to loose it,
that mushroom with its gills and ropes, the thing
with silver skin that fattened in the yard,

but I could not adjourn that onset as I slid
to touch the luminous balloon, my weight a lapse the tether
would not hold. I did not mean to climb, to grow adrift

but wafted from the fence, the patio, the house
as if I could assemble breath
from over the pylons, bridges, fallow fields

horizon to horizon, apart
from what had held, I scribbled
through the clement atmosphere, then listed

in the updraft, shifting ever eastward, ever north
above the shaggy forest-rug, the ice-skin of the pond
until the highway's pencil line became a means to cross

and though they tried to follow
my craft, resplendent fungus, refused a steady course
and lurched, a bright comportment

where no conjecture could dismantle me.

NOTES

"Shatter and Thrust as a Series of Silver Gelatin Prints"
A number of the images in this poem are in dialogue with work by photographer Gary Green.

"Self Portrait as Dido"
extremum hoc miserae det munus amanti: "Let him grant his miserable lover this one last gift: empty time . . . until fortune teaches me, defeated, how to sorrow." (The *Aenid*, Book IV).

"What She Sees When She Hushes"
Originally comprised of mesostics from Gertrude Stein's "Composition as Explanation" and "What Does She See When She Shuts Her Eyes." I am indebted to Karl Gartung for introducing me and my students to the mesostic form.

"What to Ask For, How to See"
"The error is not to fall, but to fall from no height" is from a lecture delivered by Dean Young at the 2010 Squaw Valley Community of Writers Summer Poetry Workshop.

"On the Obsolescence of Prayer"
blue has no dimensions: A quote from artist Yves Klein in his 1959 lecture at the Sorbonne: "Blue has no dimensions, it is beyond dimensions, whereas the other colours are not . . ."